W9-CPB-758

The LUNATIC

Also by Charles Simic

The LUNATIC

Poems

CHARLES SIMIC

An Imprint of HarperCollins*Publishers*

HarperCollins books may be purchased for educational, business, or sales promotional use. For information please e-mail the Special Markets Department at SPsales@harpercollins.com.

FIRST EDITION

Designed by Suet Yee Chong

Library of Congress Cataloging-in-Publication Data has been applied for.

ISBN 978-0-06-236474-6

15 16 17 18 19   OV/RRD   10 9 8 7 6 5 4 3 2

Acknowledgments

These poems were first published in the following magazines, to whose editors grateful acknowledgment is made: *The New Yorker, The New York Review of Books, Washington Square Review, Slate, The Southern Review, Salmagundi, New Republic, London Review of Books, Esquire, Literary Review,* and *The Paris Review.*

for Helen

Contents

III

I

TODAY'S MENU

All we got, mister,
Is an empty bowl and a spoon
For you to slurp
Great mouthfuls of nothing,

And make it sound like
A thick, dark soup you're eating,
Steaming hot
Out of the empty bowl.

BREEDER OF BLACK CATS

Carrying a fresh litter of them
In pockets of his overcoat
As he meanders down the street,
Letting a kitten loose here and there
To run free as a warning to me
And to everyone else in sight,
While donning his dark glasses,
Hoping not to be recognized
Entering a flower shop to buy flowers
For one or two upcoming funerals.

THE LUNATIC

The same snowflake
Kept falling out of the gray sky
All afternoon,
Falling and falling
And picking itself up
Off the ground,
To fall again,
But now more surreptitiously,
More carefully
As night strolled over
To see what's up.

O SPRING

O Spring, if I were to face a firing squad
On a day like this, I'd wear
One of your roadside flowers
Behind my ear, lift my chin high

Like a pastry cook standing
Next to a prize-winning wedding cake,
Smile like a hairdresser
Giving Cameron Diaz a shampoo.

Lovely day, you passed through town
Like a Mardi Gras parade
With ladies wearing colorful plumage on their heads
Riding on your floats,

Leaving the moon in the sky
To be our night watchman and check with its lantern
On every last patch of snow
That may be hiding in the woods.

ABOUT MYSELF

I'm the uncrowned king of the insomniacs
Who still fights his ghosts with a sword,
A student of ceilings and closed doors,
Making bets two plus two is not always four.

A merry old soul playing the accordion
On the graveyard shift in the morgue.
A fly escaped from a head of a madman,
Taking a rest on the wall next to his head.

Descendant of village priests and blacksmiths:
A grudging stage assistant of two
Renowned and invisible master illusionists,
One called God, the other Devil, assuming, of course,
I'm the person I represent myself to be.

ETERNITIES

Small store, is it only cobwebs
And shadows you sell?
I saw my pale reflection
In your dimmed-out interior

Like a gentleman burglar
Unable to make up his mind
Between a pearl necklace
And an antique clock on the wall.

Raindrops blurred the rest,
Trickling down the glass
I pressed my forehead against
As if to cool down its fevers.

LATE-NIGHT INQUIRY

Have you introduced yourself to yourself
The way a visitor at your door would?

Have you found a seat in your room
For every one of your wayward selves

To withdraw into their own thoughts
Or stare into space as if it were a mirror?

Do you have a match you can light
To make their shadows dance on the wall

Or float dream-like on the ceiling
The way leaves do on summer afternoons,

Before they take their bow and the curtain drops
As the match burns down to your fingertips?

LOOKING FOR A SOUL MATE

Recovering puff pastry and almond cookie addict,
Formerly associated with a French bakery in SoHo
And one or two choice sewers in the neighborhood
Where he learned a few deep things about life.

Reduced of late to lurking outside cheap eateries,
Concealing his twitching whiskers behind a trash can,
Or fighting with pigeons over a few popcorn,
Now seeks a comfortable brownstone free of cats,

Snap-traps and lip-smacking snacks laced with poison,
Whose wealthy owner gives lavish dinner parties,
And where he'll be free to mingle with bankers and lawyers
And sit in their wives' laps like a much-pampered pet.

THE DICTIONARY

Maybe there is a word in it somewhere
To describe the world this morning,
A word for the way the early light
Takes delight in chasing the darkness
Out of store windows and doorways.

Another word for the way it lingers
Over a pair of wire-rimmed glasses
Someone let drop on the sidewalk
Last night and staggered off blindly
Talking to himself or breaking into song.

THE WHITE LABYRINTH

There is one waiting for you,
On every blank sheet of paper.
So, beware of the monster
Guarding it who'll be invisible
As he comes charging at you,
Armed as you are only with a pen.
And watch out for that girl
Who'll come to your aid
With her quick mind and a ball of thread,
And lead you by the nose
Out of one maze into another.

STORIES

Because all things write their own stories
No matter how humble
The world is a great big book
Open to a different page,
Depending on the hour of the day,

Where you may read, if you so desire,
The story of a ray of sunlight
In the silence of the afternoon,
How it found a long-lost button
Under some chair in the corner,

A teeny black one that belonged
On the back of her black dress
She once asked you to button,
While you kept kissing her neck
And groped for her breasts.

IN ITS OWN SWEET TIME

That one remaining, barely moving leaf
The wind couldn't get to fall
All winter long from a bare tree—
That's me! thinks the old fellow,

The one they roll out in a wheelchair
So that he can watch the children
Play in the park, their mothers
Gossip all day about their neighbors

While pigeons take turns landing
And taking off from a newly arrived hearse
Parked in front of the parish church,
Dragging his gaze along as they do.

MEET EDDIE

Whose life is as merry as a beer can
Hurtling down a mountain stream
Giving some rocks a wide berth,
Bumping head-on into the others,

And going into a head-spinning twirl
Like a little girl on a piano stool,
The water shouting as it rushes past:
Are you ready to meet your Maker?

As the woods around him begin to thin
And the trees don their fright wigs
As he prepares to go over the falls
Like a blind man strapped to an accordion.

OUR GANG

Like moths
Around a streetlamp
In hell
We were.

Lost souls,
One and all.
If found,
Return to sender.

WHAT THE OLD LADY TOLD ME

He sawed my head off every night
And twice a week at a matinee performance.
Some spectators would faint,
Others would rise and applaud.

It was summer. The city was emptying
For the long holiday weekend ahead.
A newly married couple, the radio said,
Were stuck for hours in an elevator.

God's hearing aid needs a new battery,
     she told me.
There were cries for help and shouts
In the street last night, a woman
Pleading with a man to stop beating her.

It's because she sits at her window
Long after everyone else has gone to sleep
That she overhears and sees such things,
And many others too awful to mention.

NEW HAIRCUT

In a head this old and thick there are all sorts of ideas,
Some of them cockeyed, of course.
They saw wood four to a bed under a rope
Tied into a noose dangling from the ceiling.

In a head this old there is a woman undressing,
A radio singing softly to itself,
A small dog running in circles.
There's a house detective making his rounds,
Wearing a funny hat as if it were New Year's Eve.

O mysteries! Nina Delgado, the greatest of all,
Whose name I saw spray-painted on a factory wall,
And who like a leaf that has fallen far from a tree
Is now floating serenely out to sea, or back to me.

To have so many screws loose in one's head—
Is that what God and the Devil wrought?
In a head this old, there's also someone
Who every now and then peeks into a mirror
And shudders because there's no one there.

SOME LATE-SUMMER EVENING

When the wind off the lake
Stirs the trees' memories
And their dark leaves swell
Against the fading daylight
With an outpouring of tenderness—
Or could it be anguish?
Making us all fall silent
Around the picnic table,
Unsure now whether to linger
Over our drinks or head home.

II

LET US BE CAREFUL

More could be said
Of a dead fly
In the window
Of a small shed,
And of an iron typewriter
That hasn't
Lifted a key in years,
Both in delight
And dark despair.

AS YOU COME OVER THE HILL

You'll see cows grazing in a field
And perhaps a chicken or a turtle
Crossing the road in their sweet time,
And a small lake where a boy once
Threw a girl who couldn't swim,

And many large maple and oak trees
Offering ample shade to lie in,
Their branches to hang yourself from,
Should you so desire,
Some lazy afternoon or evening

When something tells the birds to hush,
And the one streetlight in the village
To keep a few moths company
And the large old house put up for sale
With some of its windows broken.

ONCE DECEMBER COMES

There's another kind of sky,
Another kind of light
Over the wintry fields,
Some other kind of darkness
Following in its footsteps,
Eager to seek our company
In these frostbitten little homes,
Standing bravely
With no dog in sight.

BARE TREES

One of my thoughts
Eloped with a leaf
The wind blew off a tree,
With two crows
Setting forth from another
In hot pursuit
Across the bleak landscape,
Like a frantic father
With a minister in tow.

THE LIGHT

Our thoughts like it quiet
In this no-bird dawn,
Like the way the early light
Takes the world as it finds it
And makes no comment
About the apples the wind
Has blown off a tree,
Or the horse broken loose
From a fenced field grazing
Quietly among the tombstones
In a small family graveyard.

NIGHT MUSIC

Little brook, running past my house,
I like the tune you hum to yourself
When night comes,
And only the two of us are awake.
You keep me company
So I don't fear
The darkness round my bed
And the thoughts in my head
Flying crookedly like bats
Between the old church and the graveyard.

DON'T NAME THE CHICKENS

Let them peck in the yard
As they please,
Or walk over to stand
At the edge of the road.

The rooster strutting about
Will keep an eye on them,
Till it's time
To withdraw under a tree,

And wait for the heat
To pass and the children
To return to the toys
They left lying in the dust.

For, come Sunday,
One of the chickens may lose its head
And hang by its feet
From a peg in the barn.

PASTORAL

Is that an uprooted root of a tree,
Or a dentist's chair in the meadow?

The cow grazing may be the nurse,
But I don't see the doc,

Unless, it's that mutt running their way
With ears flapping, wagging his tail.

AS I WAS SAYING

That fat orange cat
Slipping in and out
Of the town jail
Whenever it pleases,
How about that?

SINBAD THE SAILOR

On dark winter nights in the country,
The poor and the old keep
A single light lit in their homes,
Weak and not easy to see,
Like someone who had rowed his boat
Beyond the sight of land,
And had lowered his oars
To rest and light a cigarette
With the sea quiet around him—
Or would they be dark fields
Made quiet by the falling snow?

THE EXECUTION

It was the earliest of sunrises
And the quietest.
The birds, for reasons of their own,
Kept mum in the trees
Whose leaves remained
Calm throughout
With only a small number
In the upper branches
Sprinkled with fresh blood.

THREE COWS

These must be the cows who prayed
   to be born again
   and graze side by side
   on this pretty meadow.

And did so all summer long,
   lifting their heads only
   to look with their sad eyes
   at some poor devil like you,

who has stopped by their fence,
   wearied by some thought or other,
   and has now roused himself
   discovering he has company.

THE MISSING HOURS

Even time took a rest
On such summer afternoons
Sunning itself on a lawn
Like an unknown woman
Lying half-naked
Wearing dark glasses,
Long into the evening,
Which never seemed to come.
Only a shadow snuck
A peek now and then
From a church or a tree
And drew back in misery.

THE NEW WIDOW

Weren't you to be her prisoner for life
In her father's woodshed once?
Didn't she make you strip your shorts
And cover your eyes with one hand,
So she could touch you with the other,
Till both of your knees went weak
While a rooster kept crowing in the heat
And deep slumber of the afternoon.

THE WINE

Whatever solace you have for me,
Glass of old red wine,
Whisper it into my ear
With each little sip I take,
And only in my ear,
In this hour made solemn
By the news on the radio,
The dying fires of the sunset,
And the trees in my yard
Putting on their black coats.

IN MY GRANDMOTHER'S TIME

Death asking an old woman
To please sew him a button,
And she agrees, gets out
Of bed and starts looking
For her needle and thread
With a lit candle the priest
Had placed above her head.

BLACK BUTTERFLY

Ghost ship of my life,
Weighed down by coffins
Sailing out
On the evening tide.

III

THE STRAY

One day, chasing my tail here and there,
I stopped to catch my breath
On some corner in New York,
While people hurried past me,
All determined to get somewhere,
Save a few adrift like lost children.

What ever became of my youth?
I wanted to stop a stranger and ask.
"It went into hiding," said an old woman
Who'd read my mind.
"Swimming with sharks," a drunk concurred,
Fixing me with one bloody eye.

It was summer, and then as quietly as a bird lands,
The sidewalks were dusted with snow
And I was shivering without a coat.
I had hopes we'd meet again, I told myself,
Have a drink and recall the nights
When we used to paint this town red.

I thought you'd be in a straitjacket by now,
You'd say to me,
Making funny faces at doctors and nurses.

Instead, here you are full of fleas,
Dodging cars and buses
To follow a pair of good-looking legs home.

"And you, Judas," I summoned the strength to shout,
"Will you be coming to my funeral?"
But he was gone already. It had gotten late in the day,
Very late—and since there was nothing
That could be done about it—
I thought I'd better toddle along myself.

ON THE BROOKLYN BRIDGE

Perhaps you're one of the many dots at sunset
I see moving slowly or standing motionless,
Watching either the gulls in the sky or the barge
With a load of trash passing on the river below.

The one, whose family doesn't want to hear from,
On his way to a night class in acting, passing
An old Chinese waiter going in the opposite direction,
And a bodybuilder and a nurse holding hands.

And what about the one I'm always hoping to run into?
Though I barely remember what she looked like?
She could be one of the few that have lingered on,
Or the one that vanished since I last glanced that way.

THE ESCAPEE

The name of a girl I once loved
Flew off the tip of my tongue
In the street today,
Like a pet fly
Kept in a matchbox by a madman—
Gone!
Making my mouth fall open
And stay open,
So everyone walking past me could see.

OH, MEMORY

You've been paying visits
To that hunchbacked tailor
In his long-torn-down shop,
Hoping to catch a glimpse
Of yourself in his mirror
As he sticks steel pins
And makes chalk marks
On a small child's black suit
Last seen with its pants
Dangling from a high beam
In your grandmother's attic.

THE MEDIUM

This round table belonged to a woman
Who used to summon ghostly visitors
And transmit their cryptic messages
To her guests holding hands in a circle,
Their faces dimly lit by a candle,

Hoping to see their loved one appear,
Or at least hear the familiar voice
Greet them once again, divulge a secret
From beyond the grave,
Make someone in the room cover their ears,
Another one break into sobs,

While beyond the thick drawn curtains,
The snowflakes are starting to fall
On this cold, dark and silent night,
Each one determined to bury something
No matter how small, no matter how big.

PAST THE FUNERAL HOME

Where lives a pretty girl
Who comes and goes
Twirling her red dress
Like a Spanish dancer,
And a blind old healer
I never laid eyes on,
Who has a line of women
Waiting on the stairs
Late into the night
With their heads hung low,
Clutching their purses
Or saying a silent prayer.

SO EARLY IN THE MORNING

It pains me to see an old woman fret over
A few small coins outside a grocery store—
How swiftly I forget her as my own grief
Finds me again—a friend at death's door
And the memory of the night we spent together.

I had so much love in my heart afterward,
I could have run into the street naked
Confident anyone I met would understand
My madness and my need to tell them
About life being both cruel and beautiful,

But I did not—despite the overwhelming evidence:
A crow bent over a dead squirrel in the road,
The lilac bushes flowering in some yard,
And the sight of a dog free from his chain
Searching through a neighbor's trash can.

THE BAMBOO GARDEN

Bad luck, my very own, sit down and listen to me:
You make yourself scarce for months at a time
Making preparations for some new calamity,
Then come to shake me awake some dark night,

Wiping the sweat off your face, asking
For a glass of water, while mumbling something
About how a mixed bag of misery and laughter
Is all that I can expect from a life like mine,
While I listen, none the wiser like a blind man

Holding a fortune cookie in a Chinese restaurant
And waiting for a waiter to come along
And read it to him, but there isn't one coming,
'Cause it's late and the Bamboo Garden is closed.

WET MATCHES

Once again the short, gray days,
The low sky, the steady rain
Over these derelict neighborhoods
One catches sight of a train.

Old people hold their heads
In windows of unlit rooms.
Or withdraw quietly
To lie with their faces to the wall.

Sweet summer beyond recall,
The children are in school
Doing their wretched lessons
While their fathers play pool.

Girl in trouble and the boy to blame,
Soaked through and shivering,
Holding a wet match to her cigarette,
Here comes your bus!

AT THE JEWELER'S

A small scale accustomed to
Weighing precious stones
Sat still while he tucked
A magnifying lens in his eye.

Outside, an icy drizzle had commenced
Pelting the gray pavement.
Flocks of black umbrellas
Darkened the view of the street

As she leaned on the counter,
Muttering something about how much
That little ring means to her,
While he hastened to give it back.

DEAD TELEPHONE

Something or someone I can't name
Made me sit down to this game
I'm still playing many years later
Without ever learning its rules or finding out
Who's winning or losing,

Even as I strain my wits studying
The shadow I cast on the wall
Like a man waiting for a phone call
All night by a dead telephone
Telling himself it might still ring.

The silence around me so deep
I hear a pack of cards being shuffled,
But when I look back startled,
There's only a moth on a window screen,
Its mind like mine too wired to sleep.

OUR PLAYHOUSE

We played in the shadow
Of murderers' at work,
Kneading soldiers out of mud,
Stepping on them
When we were done playing.

Girls walking the streets
Gave us bread to eat.
An old dog with a limp
Kept us warm at night
As we huddled in doorways.

My friends, my playmates,
We never saw the dead,
Only the birds scatter
After we heard the gunshots
And ducked our heads.

VICES OF THE EVENING

Venus in a bath with cockroaches.
Everyone else hidden from view;
Their windows either dark or lit
And hung with grubby curtains.

Snow spitting out of the dark sky,
Making sidewalks treacherous,
Not even one person in sight,
Or a car moving in the street.

Imagination, Devil's old helper,
Showed me her bare breasts
Being soaped as I hurried by,
Because the wind in my face was raw.

THE FEAST

Dine in style tonight
With your misery, Adele.
Put on your silver wig
And that black dress
With plenty of cleavage,
And haughtily offer it a seat
At the head of the table,
Leaving the intimacies
That are sure to follow
This feast of empty plates
To your friend's imagination.

THE EXECUTIONER'S DAUGHTER

Waiting for her to come to me
After she's done scrubbing the bloodstains
Out of her father's shirt,
Already hearing her bare feet
On the hard floor outside of my cell,

While quickly thinking up ways
To occupy my two hands
As she steps out of her skirt,
And explain to her between kisses
How after wasting a lifetime

In devotion to various lost causes,
I found happiness in the arms
Of Death's prettiest daughter,
Tending to her bedtime needs
While I still have a head on my shoulders.

THE FLEA

What a little flea loves to see
Is two lovers undress
And jump into bed,
And be done with their lovemaking
Quickly, so it can have
Them all to itself,
As they nod off in each other's arms,
Quitting their snoring
Only to scratch themselves.

AUTUMN EVENING

Poor goldfish
Some kid threw in
A rain puddle.

No, worse than that!

Swimming
In a dead man's
Pickle jar.

Yeah, poor fish.

IN THIS PRISON OF OURS

Where the turnkey is so discreet,
No one ever sees him
Making the rounds,
It takes a brave soul
To tap on the wall of his cell
When the lights are out,
Hoping to be overheard,
If not among the angels in heaven,
Then among the damned in hell.

IV

THIS TOWN IS ALRIGHT

A little river, then a bridge,
After which a row of white homes
With well-trimmed lawns
And a fat, bowlegged dog
Walking slowly from the curb,
Carrying a paper in his mouth.

DRIVING AROUND

And then there is our Main Street
That looks like
An abandoned movie set
Whose director
Ran out of money and ideas,
Firing at a moment's notice
His entire filming crew,
And the pretty young actress
Dressed for the part
Standing with a pinched smile
In the dusty window
Of Miss Emma's bridal shop.

SUMMER EVENING

Lingered under a tree chatting with a bird
I could hear, but never did see,
While night fell and lights came on
In a few small homes along the street
Surprising a cat with something in its mouth.

In the next block, there was a travel agent
With a poster of Venice in the window
I studied for a long time in order to determine
Whether the boats on the Grand Canal
Had moved any closer to their destination.

Beyond the tracks overgrown with weeds,
There was a small, dimly lit carnival
With a merry-go-round, a shooting gallery
And a young couple trying their luck
With a rifle on a row of marching ducks,

While I rambled on, thinking, sooner or later
I'll find my way home, alone or in the company
Of some real or imaginary companion
Tapping the sidewalk with his white cane,
Or delivering Chinese food in the neighborhood.

THAT WAS SOME NIGHT

A small troop of merrymakers,
Most likely shown the door
At some party in the neighborhood
Or an after-hours dive,
Still whooping it up
As they stagger down the street
With a girl in a wedding dress
Trailing after them on bare feet
Carrying a pair of white shoes
And walking as if on eggshells,
While calling out to someone ahead:
"Hey, you! Where the fuck
Do you think you're going?"

ETERNITIES

A child lifted in his mother's arms to see a parade
And that old man throwing bread crumbs
To the pigeons crowding around him in the park,
Could they be the very same person?

The blind woman who knows the answer recalls
Seeing a ship as big as a city block
All lit up in the night sail past their kitchen window
On its way to the dark and stormy Atlantic.

THE LIGHT

Admittedly, yours is an odd
Sort of work, galactic traveler.
I watched you early this morning
Get on your knees by my bed
To help a pair of my old shoes
Find their way out of the dark.

MEMORY TRAIN

Back to Mandrake the Magician,
The man of mystery often seen
In the company of swells and
Denizens of the underworld,
While Mother kneads pie dough
And sways her hips to the radio,
And the fat, bowlegged dog
Drools over a red rubber ball,
When there is a flash of lightning
Followed by a roll of thunder
And sudden darkness upon us all.

THE HORSE

I awoke in the middle of the night to find
A horse standing quietly over my bed.
My friend, I'm so glad you're here, I said,
It's snowing and you must've been cold
And lonely in your stable down the road
With the farmer and his wife both dead.

I'll throw a blanket over you and check
If there is a lump of sugar in the kitchen,
Like the one I saw a man in a top hat
Slip to a mare in a circus, but I fear you might
Be gone when I get back, so I better stay
And keep you company here in the dark.

WITH ONE GLANCE

That mirror understood everything about me
As I raised the razor to my face.
Oh, dear God!
What a pair of eyes it had!
The eyes that said to me:
Everything outside this moment is a lie.

*

As I looked out of the window today
At some trees in the yard,
A voice in my head whispered:
Aren't they *something*?
Not one leaf among them stirring
In the heat of the afternoon.
Not one bird daring to peep
And make the hand of the clock move again.

*

Or how about the time when the storm
Tore down the power lines on our street
And I lit a match and caught a glimpse
Of my face in the dark windowpane

With my mouth fallen open in surprise
At the sight of one tooth in front
Waiting like a butcher in his white apron
For a customer to walk through his door.

*

It made me think of the way a hand
About to fall asleep reaches out blindly
And suddenly closes over a fly,
And remains tightly closed,
Listening for a buzz in the room,
Then to the silence inside the fist
As if it held in it an undertaker
Taking a nap inside a new coffin.

MIGRATING BIRDS

If only I had a dog, these crows congregating
In my yard would not hear the end of it.
If only the mailman would stop by my mailbox,
I'd stand in the road reading a letter
So all you who went by could envy me.

If only I had a car that runs well,
I'd drive out to the beach one winter day
And sit watching the waves
Trying to hurt the big rocks,
Then scattering like mice after each try.

If only I had a woman to cook for me
Some hot soup on cold nights
And maybe bake a chocolate cake,
A slice of which we'd take to bed
And share after we've done loving.

If only these eyes of mine would see better,
I could read about birds migrating
Over vast oceans and deserts
And their need to return to us every spring,
After visiting many warm and exotic countries.

SCRIBBLED IN THE DARK

Sat up
Like a firecracker
In bed,

Startled
By the thought
Of my death.

*

Hotel of Bad Dreams.

The night clerk
Deaf as a shoe brush.

*

Body and soul
Dressed up
As shadow puppets,

Playing their farces
And tragedies
On the walls of every room.

*

Oh, laggard snowflake
Falling and melting
On my dark windowpane,

Eternity, the voiceless,
Wants to hear you
Make a sound tonight.

*

Softly now, the fleas are awake.

PASSING THROUGH

An anonymous,
Inconspicuous someone,
Smaller than a flea
Snuck over my pillow last night,
Unbothered by me,
Abject and humble,
And in a rush, I bet,
To get to a church
And thank his saints.

DARK NIGHT

Because life eternal is boring,
Angels play pinochle in heaven,
Devils play poker in hell.
You can hear the cards smack the table
In the dead of the night.
God playing a game of solitaire,
Satan playing one as well,
Except he cusses and cheats.

PEEP SHOW

Behold! A snowball in hell
Next to a burning lake.
One of the devil's little imps
Is about to throw hard
At the back of some naked,
Newly damned woman
Still wearing her bridal veil.

OH, I SAID

My subject is the soul
Difficult to talk about,
Since it is invisible,
Silent and often absent.

Even when it shows itself
In the eyes of a child
Or a dog without a home,
I'm at a loss for words.

BIRDS IN WINTER

These wars of ours with their daily horrors
Of which few ever think or care about,
While others go off quietly to fight them,
Returning to their loved ones in coffins.

The early darkness making it difficult
To chase away such thoughts
Or distract oneself with a book,
Find again that passage of Thoreau

Where he speaks of the grand old poem
Called winter coming around each year
Without any connivance of ours, or perhaps
The one where he pleads to heaven

To let us have birds on days like these
With rich, colorful plumage to recall
The ease and splendor of summer days
Among the frozen trees and bushes in the yard.

A QUIET AFTERNOON

Generously donated for our use
By an unknown benefactor
Who made sure the sky is blue,
The breeze mild and caressing

As we lie in the shade of a tree,
Our eyelids heavy, our yawns
Lengthening and lengthening
In the stillness of the afternoon,

As the last leaf falls quiet
And time itself comes to a stop
With its brightly colored circus wagons
Far from any village or town.

Every card in the caravan lying facedown,
Only a horse in a field permitted
To flick his tail and a woman
Sunbathing in the nude to swat a fly.

THUS

The long day has ended in which so much
And so little had happened.
Great hopes were dashed,
Then halfheartedly restored once again.

Mirrors became animated and emptied,
Obeying the whims of chance.
The hands of the church clock moved,
At times gently, at times violently.

Night fell. The brain and its mysteries
Deepened. The red neon sign
FIREWORKS FOR SALE came on a roof
Of a grim old building across the street.

A nearly leafless potted plant
No one ever waters or pays attention to
Cast its shadow on the bedroom wall
With what looked to me like wild joy.